Spies of the Civil War

Carol Domblewski

SCHOLASTIC INC.

New York   Toronto   London   Auckland   Sydney
Mexico City   New Delhi   Hong Kong   Buenos Aires

Illustrations
William Ersland

Text copyright © 2003 by Scholastic Inc.
Illustrations copyright © 2003 by William Ersland.
All rights reserved. Published by Scholastic Inc.
Printed in the U.S.A.

ISBN 0-439-59781-1

SCHOLASTIC, SCHOLASTIC ACTION, and associated logos and designs are
trademarks and/or registered trademarks of Scholastic Inc.

LEXILE is a registered trademark of MetaMetrics, Inc.

7 8 9 10   23   12 11 10 09 08 07

Contents

Welcome to This Book

When you hear the word "spy," what do you think of? Spy Kids? Austin Powers? James Bond? Real spies aren't like that at all.

The job of a real spy is to find out information. So, real spies don't stand out. They try to blend in. Over 130 years ago, the North and the South of the United States were fighting each other. Each side used spies to find out what the other side was up to. These old-time spies didn't have cool gadgets. But they were brave and daring.

Here are their exciting stories.

Target Words Here are some words that
will help you understand a spy's dangerous work.

- **document:** a piece of paper with important
  information printed on it
  *A spy might have to steal documents from the
  other side.*

- **mission:** a special, important job
  *A spy's mission might be to find out where the
  other side's army will attack next.*

- **raid:** a sudden, surprise attack
  *Information from spies can help one side plan a
  raid on the other side.*

Reader Tips Here's how to get the most out
of this book:

- **Maps and Photos** As you read, check out
  the maps on pages 8 and 28 of this book. They
  will help you understand the Civil War and the
  two sides fighting it.

- **Cause and Effect** A cause is an event or
  action that makes something happen. An effect
  is a result of an event or action. Ask yourself
  "Why?" to find the cause. Ask yourself
  "What happened?" to find the effect.

1

An All-American War

In this war, Americans spied on each other.

During a war, getting information about the
other side can make all the difference. If you
know when and where the enemy is going to
attack, you can prepare your army. If you know
how many **troops** the enemy has, you'll know
how many you need. Getting this information
is the job of spies.

From 1861 until 1865, America was at war.
But this war was different. America was not
fighting another country. Instead, two different
parts of the United States—the North and the
South—were at war with each other.

It began in 1860 when Abraham Lincoln was
elected president. Lincoln wanted to end
slavery. But the Southern states did not. One by

one, they **seceded** and left the United States. They announced that they were starting their own country. It was called the Confederate States of America. They even elected their own president, Jefferson Davis.

President Lincoln was bitterly opposed to the South's actions. He was determined to keep the United States together. (That's why the group of states that stayed loyal to Lincoln was called the **Union.**)

In April of 1861, the Confederates went too far. They attacked a United States fort. Lincoln declared war.

For four years, the war raged on. Most people believed that their side was right. And they were willing to die for it. More than half a million soldiers were killed.

The spies of the Civil War risked their lives as well. These men and women weren't fighting, but many spies who were caught were hanged. These were people willing to die for their beliefs.

The North
"The Union"

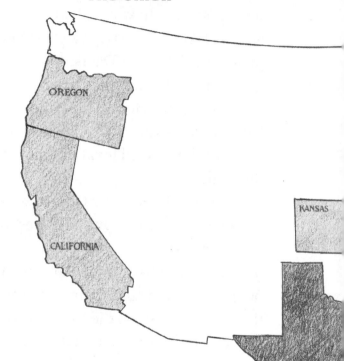

President: Abraham Lincoln
Capital: Washington, D.C.
States: Maine, New Hampshire, Vermont, Massachusetts, Rhode Island, Connecticut, New York, New Jersey, Pennsylvania, Delaware, Maryland, Kentucky, Ohio, Michigan, Indiana, Illinois, Wisconsin, Minnesota, Iowa, Kansas, Oregon, and California

MINNESOTA

MICH.

WISCONSIN

IOWA

MICHIGAN

INDIANA

OHIO

ILLINOIS

MISSOURI

KENTUCKY

NEW HAMPSHIRE
VERMONT

MAINE

NEW YORK

MASSACHUSETTS

RHODE ISLAND

PENNSYLVANIA

CONNECTICUT

NEW JERSEY

DELAWARE

MARYLAND

WASHINGTON, D.C.

WEST VIRGINIA

THE SOUTH

> **Look at the capital of the Union, Washington, D.C. Why do you think it was full of people who supported the South?**

Supporters: Unionists, also called Yankees
Goal: To keep the United States together as one country
Position on Slavery: Against it

2

Elizabeth Van Lew: Crazy for Her Cause?

A Southerner helped the North.

In Civil War days, most men wanted to be soldiers, not spies. They wanted to win honor on the battlefield. They did not want to sneak around looking for information. Also, most spies weren't paid. Soldiers were. Still, some men did spy. But many of the best spies were women.

Most people thought spy work was too dangerous for women, so female spies were rarely **suspected.** And no one would have thought that a rich woman from the South would spy for the North. But they were wrong.

Elizabeth Van Lew grew up in a wealthy family in Richmond, Virginia, but her parents sent her north to school in Pennsylvania.

Going to school in the North, Elizabeth learned to hate slavery. The first thing she did when she returned home to Virginia was free the family slaves. And when war broke out, she wanted to do something to help the North. So she decided to become a spy.

Elizabeth heard that there were Union prisoners being held in the jail in Richmond. She figured that they would have some information about what the Confederate troops were doing. She wanted to find out what the prisoners knew and tell President Lincoln.

Back then, it was a woman's place to provide help and comfort. So, Elizabeth took food and medicine to the prisoners. But Elizabeth's neighbors didn't like the idea one bit. The trouble was, Elizabeth was caring for *enemy* prisoners. Was she crazy?

Heads Up!

Elizabeth went to school in the North. How did this affect her feelings about slavery?

"Crazy Bet"

Elizabeth figured being crazy was a great cover, or disguise. So, she began to act even crazier. She dressed strangely. And she walked down the street talking to herself. Soon, everyone was calling her "Crazy Bet." Bet is a nickname for Elizabeth.

Elizabeth went to the prison day after day. She brought food and books. She asked about the prisoners' health and families. When the guards weren't listening, she would whisper, "What do you know?" And the prisoners would tell her. They told her where the Confederate troops were headed. They told her how fast the troops were moving. And they told her where the troops hid their supplies.

She also **eavesdropped** on the Confederates in charge of the prison and learned even more.

But Bet did more than listen. She also helped Union prisoners escape. First, she hid them in a secret room in her house. Then she helped them get out of the city and head to the North.

Information on the Run

At first, Elizabeth sent her news directly to President Lincoln in letters. But that quickly became too dangerous. The Richmond postmaster wondered why Crazy Bet was writing so often to the Union president.

Elizabeth started using runners instead. Sometimes, one runner would take the secret message from one point to the next, then pass it to a second runner—like a relay race. And sometimes Elizabeth would tear one message into several pieces. Each runner would go a different way and carry just one part of the message. Once all the pieces arrived, the reader would have to put them together.

Despite how careful Elizabeth was, people were getting **suspicious** of her. They started to watch her more and more closely.

┌─**Heads Up!**─────────────────
│ *What did Elizabeth do to seem crazy? How
│ did this act help her to spy?*
└──────────────────────

Sometimes Elizabeth hid secret messages inside eggs.

So "Crazy Bet" found new ways to keep her information secret. She sent her runners, dressed as servants, to the Union camps with baskets of eggs. One of the eggs would be empty and have a message inside it. Elizabeth also wrote some messages in invisible ink. Someone had to brush milk on the message to read it.

A Spy Ring

One person Elizabeth definitely wanted in her **spy ring** was Mary Bowser. Bowser had once been the Van Lews's slave. The family had freed her and sent her North to go to school. Elizabeth asked Mary to come back to Richmond as a spy. Mary said yes.

Elizabeth got Mary a job as a servant in the home of Jefferson Davis. He was the president of the **Confederacy!** Mary never let anyone know that she could read or write. She never appeared to be listening or snooping. But that's exactly what she did.

She listened in on battle planning, and she read **documents** she found around the house. She passed on all the information to Elizabeth.

By this time, Elizabeth was sending all of her information to General Ulysses S. Grant, the **commander** of the Union army. At the end of the war, Grant visited Elizabeth in Richmond. He told her that the information she sent him during the war was by far the most valuable he had received.

During the Civil War, everyone in Richmond thought Elizabeth was crazy. After the war, when the truth came out, everyone hated her for helping the North. After all, Richmond had been the capital of the Confederacy. So, Elizabeth died alone and poor. She had spent most of her money on the cause to end slavery. And no one from her hometown of Richmond came to her funeral.

Heads Up!

After the war, Elizabeth was hated by the people in her town, and she died poor and alone. Do you think she regretted spying for the North? Why or why not?

3

Timothy Webster:
The Hero Who Was Hanged

A good spy came to a bad end.

Timothy Webster had been a New York City police officer when he was asked to spy for the Union. He had already worked as a detective for the famous Pinkerton Detective Agency.

His boss, Allan Pinkerton, would be working for the Union as well. President Abraham Lincoln had asked him to run the **Secret Service.** As head of the Secret Service, Pinkerton would be in charge of all the Union spies.

Timothy had been one of Pinkerton's best detectives. Now he would become one of his best spies. President Lincoln would soon find out how good a spy Timothy could be.

Lincoln was on a train headed for Washington, D.C. The train was to make a stop in Baltimore, a city in the state of Maryland. Confederate soldiers planned to **assassinate** Lincoln once the train reached Baltimore.

Luckily, Timothy learned about this plan just in time. Lincoln's route was changed. The train did not go through Baltimore. Timothy's information had saved Lincoln's life.

Timothy began spying because he wanted to help the Union win the war. But he was a Northerner from a big city. People from the South would be suspicious of this New York Yankee. They wouldn't trust him. How could he learn their secrets?

The South's False Friend

Timothy traveled deep into the South. There he made friends with Confederate soldiers.

"Death to the Union!" he would cry. "Let's finish off those Yanks."

The Southerners believed him. One reason was that Timothy was a good actor. Another reason was that many people didn't support the side where they lived. (Remember Elizabeth Van Lew?) Some Northerners supported the South. Some Southerners supported the North.

Timothy told people in the South a part of the truth. He told them that he had been asked to spy for the North. Then he added a lie. He told them that what he really wanted to do was help the South.

Timothy was so believable that he was even made a corporal in the Southern army. He was now a **double agent**. This was a very dangerous thing to do. If he got caught, he'd be killed.

But Timothy kept up his act so well, he was invited to join a Confederate secret society. He was even asked to speak at one of their meetings. The meeting was in Ohio, a Northern state. The Confederates planned the meeting to try to get more Northerners to join their side.

Heads Up!

What did Timothy say to make Southerners believe he supported their side? What else helped Timothy fool the Southerners?

Timothy escaped the raid he helped plan.

But Timothy had his own **agenda** for the Confederate's meeting that night. He helped Union soldiers plan a **raid.**

As Timothy prepared to speak, Union soldiers surrounded the building. A signal was given and the soldiers stormed in. Many Southern leaders were captured. Timothy climbed out a window. No one ever guessed that he was working for the North. Instead, they congratulated him on his daring escape.

Webster Is Betrayed

Timothy might have gone on spying for the North for the rest of the war. But his own people betrayed him.

Two Northern spies were caught on a **mission** in the South. The Confederate soldiers pressed the spies hard for information.

"Who else is spying for the North? Tell us and we'll spare your lives."

The two spies gave the name Timothy Webster. The Confederates could hardly believe it. Timothy had fooled them completely.

Now the Confederates would get their revenge. Timothy was caught and given the death sentence. The Yankee spy would hang.

Timothy stood on the platform. The hangman put the noose around his neck and pulled tight. Timothy took his last breath—or so he thought.

But the knot on the noose came undone and Timothy fell to the ground, alive. The hangman helped Timothy back up the platform and tied the noose around his neck again. This time the knot held. And Timothy was killed. His last words were, "I suffer a double death."

Heads Up!

Why do you think the Confederates were so angry when they learned the truth about Timothy Webster?

4

The Dabneys:
It All Came Out in the Wash

A husband and wife team unfolded their secret.

The Confederate Army refused to believe that African Americans were smart or able to write. Like women, their abilities and talents were **underestimated.** That's why escaped slaves made perfect Union spies.

Very few written records of black spies in the Civil War have survived. But this one comes from a newspaper article printed in 1863. A Union officer wrote it about a husband and wife spy team.

How Does He Know?

During the war, a Southern slave named Dabney and his wife crossed a river to freedom.

The river was in Virginia and the northern bank was controlled by the Union. Dabney asked the Union army for a job. The Union army hired him as a cook and also as a servant to General Hooker. Little did they know that Dabney had a very different job in mind.

Dabney knew a lot about the area. He knew all the land features and told the Union soldiers about them. They found this helpful, but were a bit puzzled by Dabney. He was very interested in learning a Union code that was made up of flag signals. These were unusual interests for a cook and servant.

After a few weeks, Dabney's wife asked if she could go back across the river and be a personal servant to a Southern woman who was returning home. Again, the request may have seemed a bit strange, but the Union soldiers agreed to it.

As the days went by, Dabney told Union soldiers all kinds of information about what the Confederate army was doing. He knew when the army was moving, the direction they were moving in, and the number of troops involved.

The Union soldiers were amazed. They checked out every piece of information Dabney offered them. Every bit was true! But they couldn't figure out how he knew. They watched him and he never went anywhere. Dabney was always at his job. How was he getting all this information?

The Dabneys Come Clean

It turned out that Dabney had a good view from a window at General Hooker's headquarters. It faced across the river where his wife was working. Working for a Southern lady, Dabney's wife had a chance to learn what the Confederate Army was up to. Whenever she would find out new information, she would hang up laundry outside to dry. But she didn't hang it any old way. The Dabneys were using the flag signals to communicate.

Heads Up!

The Dabneys had been slaves. Explain why escaped slaves made perfect Union spies.

Mrs. Dabney hung the laundry in code.

Dabney showed General Hooker the system he had made up based on the flag code. A pair of pants hung upside down meant the army was moving west. If a white shirt was moved to the end of the line, it meant General Ambrose was moving upstream. A red shirt meant General Stonewall Jackson was involved.

General Hooker was impressed. And for as long as the Union army stayed on that riverbank, the Dabneys had jobs as spies.

Heads Up!

Would you like to be a spy? Why or why not? What qualities do you have that might make you a good spy?

The South
"The Confederacy"

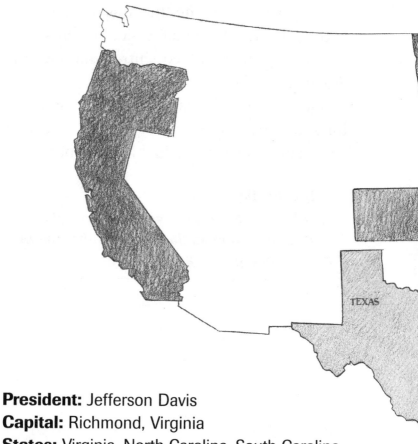

TEXAS

President: Jefferson Davis
Capital: Richmond, Virginia
States: Virginia, North Carolina, South Carolina, Georgia, Florida, Alabama, Mississippi, Tennessee, Arkansas, Louisiana, Texas

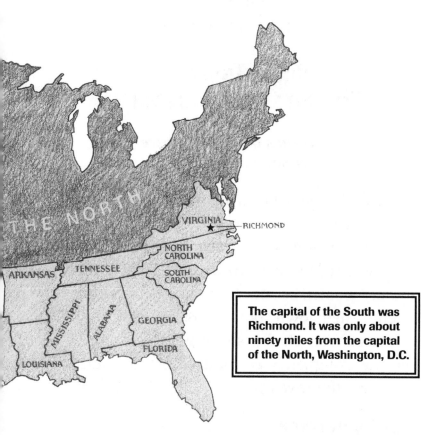

THE NORTH

VIRGINIA ★ —RICHMOND

NORTH CAROLINA

ARKANSAS　TENNESSEE

SOUTH CAROLINA

MISSISSIPPI　ALABAMA　GEORGIA

FLORIDA

LOUISIANA

> The capital of the South was Richmond. It was only about ninety miles from the capital of the North, Washington, D.C.

Supporters: Confederates, also called Rebels
Goal: To form its own country, the Confederate States of America
Position on Slavery: In favor of it

5

Belle Boyd:
Flirting with Disaster

*Belle Boyd's good looks were
her secret weapon.*

No one hired Belle Boyd to be a spy. She was a volunteer.

When the war started, the women in Belle's town watched the men go off to war. Later, some of those women became nurses. Others helped defend their own homes. Belle was only seventeen years old, but she wanted to do more. She was completely **committed** to the South and ready to prove it.

Stop Right There

Early in the war, the Union army took over Belle's hometown. Belle's father was a Confederate soldier, and he was off fighting.

So, the Boyd women were left to defend their family home.

When the Union army took over, one of the first things they did was order everyone to take down their Confederate flags and raise a Union flag in its place. But the Boyd women refused.

Union soldiers went to the Boyd home to raise the Union flag. Mrs. Boyd tried to stop them. One of the Union soldiers pushed her aside. Belle grabbed a gun and shot him!

The Union soldiers didn't fire back. They knew that in the South, it was considered a terrible **offense** to push a lady. If they had shot back, they might have had a whole town of angry people to deal with.

Belle also avoided prison. Back then, young girls were not sent to jail. But the Union soldiers did put a guard at the Boyd home.

Heads Up!

Look up the word offense *in the glossary. Why do you think that pushing a lady was considered a terrible offense?*

Belle flirted with Union soldiers to get information.

Flirting for Information

Belle wanted to help the Confederacy. She didn't know how to be a spy, but she did know how to use her beauty. That's how she got information. She began flirting with the Union men in her town. Neighbors were shocked. The Union was the enemy! But Belle was good at getting information. She found out about troop movements and secret meetings. She found out where weapons were hidden—then she stole them! She even stole medical supplies. She gave the information and the supplies to the Confederate Army.

Then one day, Belle found out about a Union meeting. She sneaked inside the house where the meeting was taking place. Then she climbed up to the attic and listened over a small hole above the meeting room. She found out some very important information about the enemy. If she could only get that information into the right hands immediately! She knew that Confederate General Stonewall Jackson was leading troops not far from her home. Belle knew what she had to do.

Bullet Holes in Her Skirts

Belle jumped on her horse and galloped across enemy fields. Bullets flew through the darkness. Some went right through her skirt.

But Belle made it to the Confederate side. She told an officer where the enemy had the fewest troops. She also told him where the next battle would be. This information helped Jackson win a battle at Front Royal, Virginia. After the battle, General Jackson wrote Belle this letter:

"I thank you, for myself and for the Army, for the great service you have done your country today.

I am your friend,

T. J. Jackson"

Captured

In time the Union figured out what Belle was doing. They locked her up, but she didn't stay in prison for long. The Union released her in exchange for some Union soldiers they wanted released from a Confederate jail. The minute she got out, she went right back to spying.

If Belle had been a man, she might have been executed. At the very least, she would have spent years in prison. But in the 1860s, men and women were treated differently. Also, women— even women spies—were not taken very seriously. And prison was a very serious place.

The Union officers had warned Belle to stop spying. They had also told her she could never cross Union **lines** again. But Belle didn't listen.

A Hero

In the South, Belle was treated like a hero. General Jackson made her an **honorary** captain in the army! A year later, Belle was put in prison again for going behind enemy lines. As soon as she was released, she started spying again!

Belle kept spying even when she got very sick with typhoid fever. Confederate doctors told her to stop spying. But she didn't.

---**Heads Up!**---

How would you describe Belle? Think of a quality that she had. Then find an example in the text that proves it.

Belle was arrested once again. This time, the Union put her on a ship and sent her to England. When she tried to return to America, a surprising thing happened. She was captured and fell in love with the Union officer who was in charge of bringing her back to America. The officer, Samuel Hardinge, let Belle escape to Canada. He was kicked out of the Navy, but he and Belle met up again in England and were married.

Finally, Belle's spying days were over. In England, she became an actress and wrote a book about her experiences. It was called *Belle Boyd in Camp and Prison.*

Altogether, Belle was arrested six or seven times. She was put in prison twice and reported as a spy at least 30 times. But she was never hung. She died from another attack of typhoid.

6

Thomas N. Conrad: A Shady Character

Thomas N. Conrad would have done anything to hurt the North.

Thomas N. Conrad was a college professor living in the Union capital of Washington, D.C. But he loved the South. And living in Washington made it easy for him to gather all kinds of information. With this information, he could do a lot of good for the South—and a lot of damage to the North.

Secret Operations

Thomas taught at Georgetown College. The dorm room windows at the college faced the Potomac River. Southern soldiers were camped just on the other side of the river. Thomas made up a code using the window shades.

Thomas asked his students to raise and lower their shades to send information about the Union to the Confederate army.

The window shade code was discovered and Thomas was arrested. But he wasn't kept in prison for long. As soon as he got out, he switched jobs. He became a **chaplain** in the Confederate army. A chaplain gives spiritual comfort to soldiers.

As a chaplain, Thomas was allowed to cross into the North to visit Southern prisoners. It was the perfect cover for a spy. Thomas was a chaplain for several months. Then he decided he could do more back in Washington, D.C.

Going back to Washington would be risky for Thomas. A lot of people already knew that he was a Southern supporter. So, Thomas gave himself a new look. He dressed differently. He changed his hair and beard. He even learned

Heads Up!

Why did Thomas change his look? Do you think he succeeded?

Thomas asked his students to lower their shades to send secret messages to Southern soldiers.

how to chew his tobacco a different way. Then he went to work. But the Confederacy didn't support all he tried to do for them.

Spying at the War Department

Thomas wanted to assassinate one of the Union generals. He chose General Winfield Scott. Thomas got a gun and made plans. But the Confederate government said no. Thomas followed orders but he did not give up spying.

Thomas went to the War Department—the Union War Department, that is. Some friends of the South were already working there. They let him into the building.

Thomas would show up at lunchtime. That's when the War Department clerks left their desks to eat. But the clerks didn't bother to put their work away. All their plans and papers were just sitting on their desks.

Thomas collected lots of information this way. At one point he gave all the Union battle plans to the Confederates! It was some of the most successful spy work of the Civil War.

The next move Thomas planned was a daring plot to kidnap President Lincoln. Again, the Confederate government said no.

The Last Disguise

After the war ended, Thomas decided to look for a job in the North. He disguised himself again. Unfortunately, his disguise made him look like a well-known criminal. So, Thomas was arrested again—and then let go again! Finally, he became the president of a college. That must have been pretty dull work compared with his earlier jobs.

Heads Up!

The Confederate government didn't want Thomas to try to kidnap Lincoln. Why do you think they were against this plan?

7

After the War

The spies faded away into history.

In the end, the North won the Civil War. The Union took over Richmond, the South's capital city. Many Southerners cried that day. Elizabeth Van Lew cheered. She flew her Union flag.

The Civil War was bloody and terrible. About 620,000 soldiers died. Many fathers, sons, and husbands were gone forever. Others carried wounds for the rest of their lives.

Five days after the war ended, there was one more **casualty**. President Lincoln was assassinated by John Wilkes Booth at the Ford Theater in Washington, D.C. This was a great loss for a country that was trying to recover after the war.

The South had been hit hard. Many homes and farms were destroyed. Entire cities were burnt to the ground. A whole way of life was gone forever. During the war, Lincoln had declared that the slaves were free. But they still weren't treated as equals. Plenty of hard times were ahead.

After the war, the spies tried to go back to having normal lives. Belle Boyd became an actress in England. Thomas Conrad returned to working at colleges. But Elizabeth Van Lew ended up poor and all alone. Her neighbors never forgave her for being a spy. Near the end of her life, she said, "No one will walk on the same street with me."

Heads Up!

When the war was over, do you think the spies were glad that they had fought for their cause?

Glossary

agenda (*noun*) a plan or list of things to be done (p. 21)

assassinate (*verb*) to kill, usually for a political reason (p. 18)

casualty (*noun*) a death related to war (p. 42)

chaplain (*noun*) a person who leads religious services and counsels people (p. 38)

commander (*noun*) leader (p. 16)

committed (*adjective)* feeling devoted to or believing in fully (p. 30)

Confederacy (*noun*) the group of Southern states that fought the Union (p. 15)

document (*noun*) a piece of paper with important information printed on it (p. 15)

double agent (*noun*) a spy who collects information for one side by pretending to be a spy for the other side (p. 19)

eavesdrop (*verb*) to secretly listen to what others are saying (p. 12)

honorary (*adjective)* given out of respect, not earned in the usual ways (p. 35)

lines (*noun*) battle area (p. 35)

mission *(noun)* a special, important job (p. 21)

offense (*noun*) a terrible insult (p. 31)

raid (*noun*) a sudden, surprise attack (p. 21)

secede (*verb*) to break away from one nation and start a separate one (p. 7)

Secret Service (*noun*) a government agency that collects information (p. 17)

spy ring (*noun*) an organized group of spies, often under the direction of one person (p. 15)

suspect *(verb)* to think someone is guilty (p. 10)

suspicious *(adjective)* feeling that someone is doing something wrong (p. 13)

troop *(noun)* a group of soldiers (p. 6)

underestimate *(verb)* to think that something is not as good as it really is (p. 23)

Union (*noun*) the group of Northern states that joined together to fight the Confederacy (p. 7)

Index